S0-BRL-174

NOAH
AND
THE RAINBOW

NOAH
AND
THE RAINBOW

written by

SHOSHANA LEPON

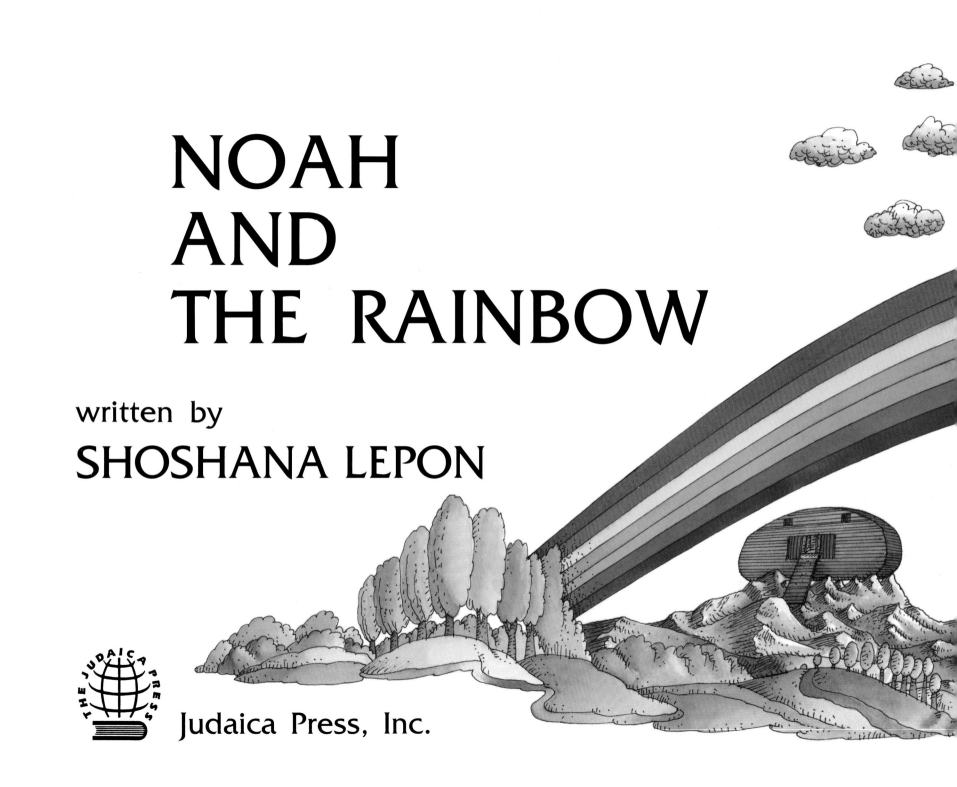

Judaica Press, Inc.

illustrated by

AARON FRIEDMAN

DEDICATED

TO

DR. ALVIN AND DR. BETTY STERN

FOR THEIR CONSTANT SUPPORT

OF THE

DIASPORA YESHIVA DAY SCHOOL

MOUNT ZION, JERUSALEM

Library of Congress Cataloging-in-Publication Data

Lepon, Shoshana.
    Noah and the rainbow / by Shoshana Lepon : illustrated
by Aaron Friedman.
          p.   cm.
    Summary: a retelling in verse of the Old Testament story
about the survival of Noah, his family, and animals during forty days
and nights of rain.
    ISBN 1-880582-04-X—ISBN 1-880582-05-8 (pbk.)
    1. Noah (Biblical figure)—Juvenile literature.   2. Noah's ark—Juvenile
literature.   3. Bible stories, English—O.T. Genesis.
[1.Noah (Biblical figure)   2. Noah's ark.   3. Bible stories—O.T.]
I. Friedman, Aaron, ill.   II. Title.
BS580.N6L37   1993   92-26431 √
222'.1109505—dc20   CIP
                                                               AC

© Copyright 1993
The Judaica Press, Inc.
New York, NY

Library of Congress Catalog Card Number 92-26431
ISBN 1-880582-04-X (hardcover)
ISBN 1-880582-05-8 (softcover)

All rights reserved
including the right
of reproduction
in whole or in part
in any form whatsoever.

Printed in Singapore

Long, long ago
In a world still new
Lived Noah, a good man
When good men were few.

5

His neighbors were wicked
And selfish and cruel.
They stole from the children
Who were walking to school.

They got into trouble
They cheated and cursed.
But their leaders did nothing
For they were the worst!

Said God: "Why should I
Keep them healthy and strong
When they use all their strength
To do things that are wrong?

"What pleasure have I
From such miserable men?
I'll bring down a flood
And start over again!"

7

God saw but one family
Bearing no blame—
Noah, his wife, and sons,
Ham, Yafet, and Shem.

8

God called out to Noah:
"Start building an ark!
Build it sturdy and strong
From thick gopher bark.

"A great flood is coming,
But I'll save your lives—
You and your sons,
And all of the wives."

9

Far from the sea
Noah built his new boat.
It looked mighty silly
With no place to float.

The people were curious,
"What's the boat for?"
"It's a warning," said Noah,
"Don't sin anymore.

"Unless you begin
To change your bad ways,
God will bring a great flood—
Forty nights, forty days."

But the people made fun
Of the words Noah spoke.
They called the great flood
A preposterous joke.

So the rain began falling—
At first it fell lightly—
To give them more time
To begin to act rightly.

But the people laughed more
As the waters poured down,
For no one believed
They were going to drown.

Just the animals understood
That this was no game.
And they all came to Noah,
Ham, Yafet, and Shem.

11

At God's command
The beasts entered in pairs—
Two lions, two lizards,
Two beetles, two bears.

Two tigers and two turtles,
Two elephants with trunks
Two puppies, two peacocks,
And even two skunks.

Of beasts for an offering,
More were needed, for sure.
So, Noah took fourteen
Of those that were pure.

He took fourteen bulls,
Fourteen sheep with thick coats,
Fourteen grey turtledoves,
And fourteen young goats.

And when the last creature
Was safe in the ark,
The mighty rains fell,
And the heavens grew dark.

The seas overflowed;
The floodwaters swirled;
And a huge, rushing wave
Rolled over the world.

It swept off one thief
Sneaking out of a house,
And knocked down two girls
Fighting over a blouse.

And three lazy boys
Who were lying in bed,
And four stingy men
Who would not share their bread.

And five people boasting,
And six telling lies—
All were lost as the waters
Continued to rise.

The flood bubbled up
Out of boiling hot fountains,
Filling the valleys
And covering the mountains.

15

And Noah felt sad
As the waters grew high
For his wicked neighbors
Would now have to die.

Yet, they could have been saved
Even on that last day
Before the great flood
Washed their evil away.

16

But no one would listen,
It seemed such a shame
To Noah, Ham, Yafet,
And the oldest son, Shem.

Noah turned to his family:
"There's so much to do.
The zebras are hungry,
The pelicans, too!

"The cows must have corn,
And the horses need hay,
And the cats want their cream
Put out fresh every day.

"The giraffes have complained
That the ceiling's too low.
They can't find a place
For their long necks to go.

"A report has come in
That the porcupine pair
Left quills poking out
Of the chimpanzee's chair.

"And the buffalo says
We must really be stricter.
He's been fighting off hugs
From the boa constrictor!

19

"From eagle to kangaroo,
Ostrich to bear
God's given these living things
Into our care.

"All the earth's creatures
Are here in our hands
And we must look after them
The best that we can."

20

Noah and his family
Did not get much sleep
With all of the animals
They had to keep.

While the monkeys were messy,
The hens kept things neat
The mice wanted quiet,
But the lambs liked to bleat.

Some beasts felt cold
And complained they would freeze
While others were so hot
They begged for a breeze.

And then there were creatures
Who slept in the day
And woke when the night came
All ready to play!

22

Noah worked hard
To keep all the beasts tame
With help from the wives,
And Ham, Yafet, and Shem.

The work never stopped,
There was always some chore—
Like cleaning the cages
Or scrubbing the floor.

And they had to run quickly
To patch up the deck
Whenever the woodpeckers
Started to peck.

23

And so if the feedings
Began a bit late
Some of the animals
Just had to wait.

Well, that might not bother
A hippo or cow,
But a lion who's hungry
Must have his food now!

24

Once, Noah was slow
To serve him his meal
So, the lion repaid Noah
By striking his heel.

From that day on
Good Noah was lame,
With more work for Ham, Yafet,
And the oldest son, Shem.

25

On Mount Ararat
The ark finally stood
And a raven was sent out
To see what it could.

The bird saw just water
In every direction,
And so he flew back
To the ark for protection.

26

After the raven
A dove went to scout.
At first also she
Could find nothing about.

Seven days later
The dove again free
Returned with the leaf
Of a green olive tree.

Said Noah: "The waters
Are surely subsiding,
But only the treetops
Have come out of hiding."

27

But still Noah waited
For God's next command:
"Leave the ark and have children,
And fill up the land."

Then for a third time
The dove made her flight.
She never looked back
As she soared out of sight.

Said Noah: "The dove
Must be building her nest.
She surely has spotted
A good place to rest."

Then out of the ark
All the animals came
With Noah, the wives,
And Ham, Yafet, and Shem.

They remembered how people
Had chosen to sin.
Now nothing remained
Where their cities had been.

29

They sacrificed birds,
Bulls, rams, and goats
To thank God for keeping them
Safe in their boat.

And God made a promise:
"Never again
Shall I flood the whole earth
To destroy all bad men.

"This rainbow you see
In the heavens above
Shall shine as a sign
Of my mercy and love."

And so we bless God
Who's the King of all kings
When we see the rainbow
He faithfully brings.

We promise to learn
From Noah's kind ways
And not be like the people
Who lived in his days.

To take care of God's world
And be just the same
As Noah, a good man,
Ham, Yafet, and Shem.

31

DID YOU KNOW?

Noah took 120 years to build the ark. First he planted a forest. When the trees had grown tall, Noah cut them down and made them into boards. He sanded the boards, measured them, and cut them into different sizes. He began to build the ark in a large field. Of course, he attracted a lot of attention. People asked him why he was doing all this. Each time, Noah told them about the flood and warned them to stop sinning; and for 120 years, the people just laughed. *Rashi, Midrash Rabbah*

Noah knew the Torah even before it was given. How do we know this? If Noah had not already studied the Torah, he would not have known which animals were pure and which were not. *Rashi*

The flood waters did not only rain down from the heavens. Boiling water also burst forth from springs deep in the earth. Most of these springs were sealed up after the flood, but a few were left open by God. Even today we find hot springs in many parts of the world. *Rashi*

Although none of the fish were taken into the ark, they did not die in the boiling flood water either. This was a miracle from God. *Rashi*

The rains continued for forty days and forty nights, but it took a full year before the water had soaked into the earth and Noah, his family, and the animals could leave the ark. *Rashi*

Whenever we see a rainbow, we say a special blessing and remember God's promise to Noah never to destroy the whole world by flood again. The blessing is:

Blessed Are You, Hashem, Our God, King of the Universe,
Who Remembers the Covenant, Is Faithful in His Covenant, and Fulfills His Word.

בָּרוּךְ אַתָּה ה׳ אֱלֹקֵינוּ מֶלֶךְ הָעוֹלָם, זוֹכֵר הַבְּרִית, וְנֶאֱמָן בִּבְרִיתוֹ, וְקַיָם בְּמַאֲמָרוֹ.

TEMPLE ISRAEL LIBRARY